Pruning

FOR

Fruit

First published 1993
Reprinted 2003
Revised edition 2008

ISBN 0 7590 1064 1

Copyright © 1993

Produced in Adelaide, South Australia:

Book and cover design by DESIGNHAUS

Illustrations by Gilbert Dashorst

Printed by Finsbury Green

Image Credits:

© *Dreamstime.com images by:*
Cover (© Amlet, © Barbara Helgason, © Joe Gough,
© Les Cunliffe, © Lgrig, © Vincent Giordano
& © Marek Mnich), pp2 © Nikola Hristovski,
pp4 © Tim Nichols & © Les Cunliffe,
pp5 © Svlumagraphica & © Andrzej Tokarski,
pp13 © Marek Mnich, pp14 © Lindsay Noechel &
© Jitkaunv, pp17 © Anna Ceglińska, pp31 © Liane
Matrisch, pp43/45 © Salahudin, pp51 © Ruslan Kokarev,
pp56 © Milosluz, pp62 © Johannes Gerhardus
Swanepoel, pp66 © Ryan Pike , pp70 © Liane Matrisch
pp71 © Robyn Mackenzie, pp72 © Peter Krautscheid

© *Adelaide Botanic Gardens images by:*
Steve Gee & Bruce Morphett

A concise guide to the care and pruning
of common fruits and vines

Pruning

FOR

Fruit

BRUCE MORPHETT

**Government
of South Australia**

Department for
Environment and Water

Board *of the*
Botanic Gardens *and*
State Herbarium

Contents

Introduction

This second addition of *Pruning for Fruit* is slightly expanded to include some basic information on planning, preparation, establishing and caring for fruit trees and vines along with brief notes on container grown fruit.

We are fortunate in Australia that we can grow a wide range of fruit trees and vines. The climate is favourable and soils are reasonable. A great benefit is that apart from fruit fly in some areas, we have few serious pests and diseases such as fireblight which would prevent us from growing our own fruit without extraordinary measures.

Pruning is a skill which anyone can master. Like all skills it involves learning and understanding some basic principles followed by lots of practice. When pruning one type of tree has been mastered, the same basic skills can be transferred to other trees and vines, with due consideration to individual growth and fruiting habit.

The advice and information available about how to prune fruit trees is often conflicting and contradictory, leaving many gardeners confused and unsure how to proceed. Some employ gardening services sometimes with disappointing results.

Opinions regarding the correct way to prune fruit trees vary enormously. This partly reflects the changes in pruning practices over time. Pruning practices earlier in the last century placed heavy emphasis on preconceived ideas of tree form; formality, symmetry and balance took precedence. Such rigid training required heavy cutting, often into vigorous and fruiting wood. A common result was stunted, disease prone trees which often produced only a fraction of the crop of which they where capable.

Experience and study conducted in fields such as plant physiology, forestry and horticulture in the last 70 or so years have greatly increased knowledge and understanding of plant growth and responses. From this, pruning principles have been developed which account for natural habit and growth.

The aim of this book is to give some basic information on fruit tree and vine growing, explain basic pruning principles and set down some guidelines, describe some ways trees and vines can be trained and outline the pruning of individual fruits.

Growing fruit

How well your fruiting trees an vines perform involves factors both within and out of your control. However, disasters notwithstanding, there are some fundamentals to follow in getting the best results from your fruit trees and vines. They are as follows:

Plan to incorporate fruiting plants into your garden plan. Decide what and how many to grow and the training method. Keep in mind to choose only varieties suitable for your climate and soils.

Choose the site carefully and prepare thoroughly.

Buy healthy, good quality varieties from a reputable source.

Plant correctly and at the appropriate time.

Care for and train young plants appropriately in their early years.

Manage and care for trees for best results throughout their productive life.

Consider lifecycle planning. At what point will the trees or vines be removed and replaced.

Planning and preparation

Fruit trees and plants can be grown in a dedicated area of the garden or incorporated into the general garden layout. Many can become a feature in the garden. What can be more attractive than the fragrant flowers of a citrus, or a shady casimiroa or walnut ?

Space requirements depend on the type of tree and the training method. Single and multiple planted trees are normally spaced 3-3.5 metres apart. Spacings for hedgerows and trellising vary from 1-3 metres. See sections on individual fruits for details.

Cross pollination is important in some fruits. See individual fruits for details.

Rootstocks enable some fruits to be grown under a wider range of soil and sometimes climatic conditions, and to impart disease and pest tolerance or resistance.

Microclimate

Most fruit trees need an open, sunny position sheltered from winds. Frost will limit the growing of evergreens and some early flowering deciduous fruits. Check to see whether your desired fruit is growing in your local area. In cooler areas, where land is sloping, a north-easterly aspect will accumulate more heat.

Soils

Fruit trees vary in their adaptability to different soils. Most thrive in well drained loams 40-50 cm deep, free of root competition from other trees. Soil reaction should be between pH 6 and pH 8.

Preparing the site

Prepare the site in autumn for winter or spring planting. Dig over an area of about a square metre and 30 cm deep for each tree. When planting trees in lawn, prepare a circle of at least 1 metre and preferably 2 metres in diameter, to avoid competition from the lawn.

Incorporate organic materials if desired and gypsum at 2 kg per square metre if the soil is hard setting. Where soil is acidic (below ph 5.5-6) use 300-400 grams per square metre lime or dolomitic lime instead of gypsum. Avoid planting into very heavy clay and limestone layers. Where topsoil is less than 25-30 cm deep, or drainage is doubtful, increase soil depth to 40-50 cm with a sandy loam. A level 6x4 trailer load for each planting site is usually enough.

Establishing young trees

Buying trees

Deciduous trees are field grown and delivered 'bare-rooted' to retail plant outlets during late autumn and early winter. Nurseries often pot surplus trees for sale later into the spring and summer. Avoid these 'potted on' trees. They have often had their roots excessively pruned to fit in the pot or bag. Evergreens including citrus are container grown and are available much of the year. Buy healthy, well grown trees free of damage with plenty of roots and keep them thoroughly moist between purchase and planting.

Planting

Plant deciduous trees soon after purchase; before mid-July for almonds and mid-August for others. Mid-Spring is the best time to plant evergreens with early Autumn being the second choice.

Prepare the planting hole at least for twice the width of the roots and a little deeper, say 50 cm wide by 30 cm deep. Break up the soil in the bottom of the hole. Measure out two cups of gypsum and half a cup of complete fertiliser (or 1-1½ cups of organic fertiliser). Sprinkle a little of each into the hole. Mix the remainder thoroughly into the soil from the hole.

Examine the roots of deciduous trees. Trim off any broken roots. With container grown evergreens like citrus, remove the tree from its container and soak in water for 10 minutes or so. Then gently tease out and untangle the roots, especially around the base of the root ball, trimming off any badly matted and tangled roots. The potting mix which falls away can be mixed with the soil from the hole.

Position the tree centrally in the hole, at the same level as previously planted. While keeping the roots spread out all around, backfill the hole with soil, firming it down as you go. Check that the tree is at the correct level.

Water the tree by forming a 5-10 cm high rim just outside the original hole, to retain the water. Flood with 10-20 litres of water to consolidate the soil around the roots and drive out air pockets.

Staking trees is normally unnecessary. Tree trunks grow thicker and stronger when allowed to flex naturally. Stakes are needed only for vines and apples on some dwarfing rootstocks. If staking is desired, place two stakes 10 cm either side and loop flexible ties to the tree.

Pruning of young deciduous fruit trees at planting is necessary to compensate roots lost in transplanting from the nursery. Evergreens generally need some pruning to shape. Refer to sections on shape and training, and individual fruits.

Care in the first year

Young fruit trees and vines which establish quickly and grow vigorously in their first year become stronger and more productive.

Protection

For the first year after planting, protect the young trunk and branches from sun damage by painting with a cheap, water based, white house paint. If the site is at all windy, protect the trees on the windward side with a shelter of a windbreak fabric, hessian or shadecloth.

Mulch

Mulch with straw or compost 5 cm or so deep. Delay mulching until October when planting in frost prone areas.

Watering

Watering of newly planted trees can vary from nil after rain, to 20 litres weekly in cool weather, to 10-20 litres every second day in hot summer weather.

Fertilisers

Early each month from September until February, apply a 20 ml measure (level tablespoon) of complete fertiliser or a quarter cup of organic fertiliser. Apply the fertiliser to a moist soil, rake the surface lightly and water in immediately.

Caring for established trees

Soil

Keep cultivation under fruit trees to a minimum to allow roots to utilise the surface soil. Maintain a 5 -10 cm deep mulch of leaves, chippings or similar coarse organic residue. A mulch will conserve moisture, minimise weed growth, moderate soil temperature, protect soil structure, encourage earthworms and will add humus to the soil as it decomposes. Keep mulch clear of the trunk to minimise the danger of trunk or collar rots.

Keep lawn at least a metre away from the trunk and preferably to the edge of the canopy or 'drip line'. Some shallow rooted garden plants even bulbs, can be grown under the trees, but avoid agressive ground-covers.

Take care when using herbicides near fruit trees. Those containing glyphosate are generally safe. Use as directed and keep away from foliage or bark. Spray only when no rain is forecast and avoid watering for 2-3 days to avoid possible root absorbtion.

Watering

To produce their best, trees need uniform moisture in their root-zone throughout the season. The most critical periods are during flowering and fruit set in spring and during the most rapid fruit development. Watering needs will vary from nil in a normal winter, to hundreds of litres per week in mid-summer.

The following table gives a rough guide to minimum weekly water requirements. It applies to well mulched trees, watered at night through drip irrigation, given annual rainfall of 500-800 mm and a dry summer. Conditions common in southern Australia. Make adjustments where your conditions vary significantly from these. Water can be applied through a sprinkler under the tree, or via micro-sprays or drippers as part of a fixed watering system.

Water in the early morning or at night, especially during summer. Watch the weather forecasts and water before the onset of hot weather.

Weekly minimum water needs (litres) for productive fruit trees.
Tree size is the average of height and width in metres.

Tree (metres)	Oct	Nov	Dec	Jan	Feb	Mar	Apr
1	17	22	25	30	26	20	12
1.5	40	50	60	65	60	45	30
2	70	90	100	110	105	80	50
2.5	110	140	160	175	160	120	75
3	155	200	230	250	235	175	110
3.5	210	270	310	340	320	240	150
4	275	355	405	440	415	310	195

Fruit maturity, harvesting and storage

Maturity

Most fruits are mature when they have reached full size and their skin background colour changes from green to the characteristic colour for that fruit. Generally, fruit is picked when it has reached full ripeness and is most palatable to eat. The main exceptions are the pome fruits, apples and European pears which are harvested at maturity, then ripen further off the tree. Avocados are also harvested while firm, then can be stored for a period before becoming soft for eating.

Harvesting

Fruit are best harvested in the early morning when they are cool and fully turgid. Check trees daily for ripe fruit. Handle fruit carefully to avoid bruising and skin damage. Most fruit should be placed in the refrigerator as soon as practical, except fruit for immediate consumption.

Storage

Store fruit requiring refrigeration in supermarket fruit and vegetable bags or similar to minimise moisture loss. Do not store fruit in clear plastic bags or plastic food wrap.

Broadly, optimum storage temperatures for fresh fruit are:

Pome fruits 0 -1°C

Stone fruits, grapes and lemons 1 - 4°C

Citrus except lemons 7-10°C

Tropical and subtropical fruits 10 -15°C

Fertilisers

Fruit trees, like all plants need adequate nutrition to grow and produce fruit. Plants must manufacture their own 'food' and it is generally accepted that there are at least 15 basic elements essential for plant growth. Of these, carbon, hydrogen and oxygen come from air and water. The rest must be supplied from the soil. These include nitrogen, phosphorus, potassium, calcium, magnesium, sulphur, manganese, iron, zinc, copper, boron and molybdenum. Others believed to be required in minuscule amounts include. chlorine, nickel, aluminium, sodium, cobalt, vanadium, and silicon. Many of these occur already in adequate amounts in the soil.

Adequate amounts of all these nutrients in correct proportions are necessary to grow healthy trees and produce fruit in the desired numbers, size and quality. Adequate fertilising is particularly important in very sandy soils as nutrients are readily leached from the root-zone by rainfall and watering.

Approximate minimum fertiliser (kilograms dry weight per tree per year).
Amounts are based on 20-25 grams nitrogen per square metre.
These need to be increased by 50% for lemons and sandy soils.
Tree size is the average of height and width in metres.

Tree size	Mixed fertiliser		Organic fertiliser		Compost
(metres)	N 10%	N 8%	N 5%	N 3%	N 1-2%
1.0	0.16-0.2	0.2-0.25	0.3-0.4	0.5-0.65	1.5-4
1.5	0.35-0.44	0.44-0.55	0.7-0.9	1.2-1.5	3.5-9
2.0	0.63-0.8	0.8-0.98	1.2-1.6	2.1-2.6	6-15
2.5	1.0-1.2	1.2-1.5	2.0-2.5	3.3-4.1	10-25
3.0	1.4-1.8	1.8-2.2	2.8-3.5	4.7-4.9	15-35
3.5	2.0-2.4	2.4-3.0	3.8-4.8	6.4-8.0	20-50

Pests, diseases and disorders

The damage and loss of the fruits of your labour caused by pests, diseases and disorders is always disappointing. Once a crop is lost, there is a 12 month wait before another develops. Some fruits are prone to a range of problems, and in order to harvest a good crop, regular prevention and control measures are required. On the other hand, others are relatively problem free and so require little or no controls.

To reduce the overall burden of problems, maintain healthy trees and vines with adequate watering, mulching and fertilising.

Reduce disease problems by collecting fallen fruit daily. Bury spoiled fruit covering with at least 100 mm of soil. Remove diseased and dead wood during the season and at winter pruning. Dispose of all suspected diseased material. Use appropriate controls where indicated.

Minimise pests by removing host plants, including weeds. Encourage the natural enemies of pests by using sprays only when necessary for acceptable crops.

Look under introductions of fruit groups for some information on specific problems. For detailed information on pests, diseases and disorders of fruits refer to publications under *Further Reading*.

Container grown fruit

Most fruit trees will grow in containers. Most suitable are those with fairly compact root systems. However, trees with vigorous roots such as some stone fruits and pear on pear roots tend to outgrow their containers fairly quickly.

The following are well worth trying:

Dwarf peach and nectarine, apples on dwarfing rootstocks M9 and M26, pear on quince rootstock, quince, loquat, passionfruit, brambles, citrus on Trifoliata or Flying Dragon rootstock, avocado, olive, pomegranate, cherry guava, feijoa, fig and mulberry.

Containers

Most large containers are suitable. 50 litres (46cm diam. x 31cm deep) is a practical minimum volume. 100 litres (60 cm diam x 36 cm deep) or larger is even better, such as half wine barrels, large concrete and terracotta pots. Check that containers have several adequate drainage holes 2cm or more in diameter.

Cut a piece of shadecloth to cover the bottom to retain the potting mix but still allowing good drainage through the large holes.

Mix

A quality potting mix is best for smaller tubs. For larger tubs and planter boxes, special loamy sand/compost mixes available from garden soil suppliers are quite suitable. They are cheaper than potting mix. Make sure they contain no heavy loam.

Potting

Prepare the tree as described previously under planting. Partially fill the container with mix and consolidate to position the tree with the stem base just below the container rim. Allow a centimetre or so for watering. Note the volume in litres of potting mix used. This is useful information when calculating fertiliser amounts.

Repotting

Trees in large containers should not need repotting, unless an inferior mix or garden soil has been used previously. Check the pH range is 5.5-6.5, and flush with a very heavy watering at the end of summer to remove salts accumulated from fertilisers and watering.

Watering

Water liberally during the warmer months, especially during hot weather. During winter and cooler months, watering will be less. Monitor the moisture regularly to gauge watering needs. A mulch of straw or similar over the top of the pot will reduce evaporation and moderate pot temperatures in summer.

Fertilising

Suitable fertilisers include soluble, controlled release, organic and mineral fertilisers. A good strategy is to use controlled release in early spring and early autumn. When using mineral fertilisers in containers, be careful to accurately measure quantities. For a fertiliser with 8-10 % N, for each litre of pot volume, apply 1 gram in early spring and 1 gram in early autumn. The quantities for a 100 litre tub therefore, are 100 grams (half a cup) on each occasion. Sprinkle fertiliser, scratch into the surface, then water immediately.

Training shaping, and pruning

Container grown trees will be much smaller due to root restriction, but training is essentially the same as for those in the ground. Establish the lower branches 50 cm or so from the base. Try to maintain a central leader. This will result in a stronger, more compact tree which is easier to manage. Refer to training and pruning for individual fruits.

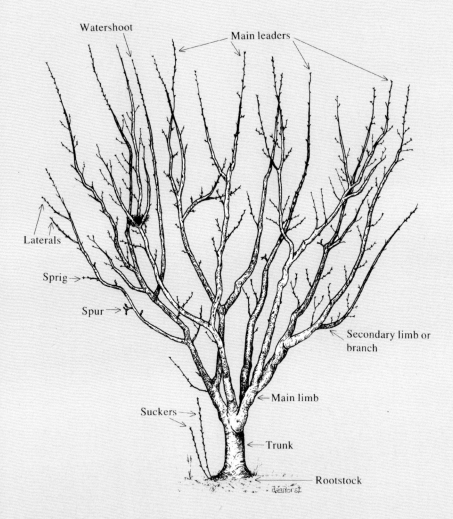

Watershoot

Main leaders

Laterals

Sprig →

Spur →

Secondary limb or
branch

Main limb

Suckers →

Trunk

Rootstock

Fig 1
Typical open centre fruit tree (plum).
*Shown in winter with an upright growth
habit showing the main parts.*

The basics

What is pruning and why do it?

Fruit trees do not have to be pruned to produce fruit. Fruit bearing is a natural and automatic consequence of growth. In fact unpruned trees crop very well, particularly when young. However, eventually a number of things happen. Trees will become too large and hard to manage, becoming overcrowded with unproductive wood. Fruit will be borne increasingly higher in and on the outer margins the tree. Cropping in some trees may be erratic; heavy crops of small fruit some years and little or none in others.

Pruning then may be described as selective removal of plant parts to manipulate and control their growth to our purposes. With fruit trees the principal aim is to assist in producing consistent crops of fruit of desirable size and quality, on a tree or plant which is convenient to manage.

The 3 R's of pruning

Pruning fulfils 3 basic functions in manipulating fruit trees.

(a) Redirect

Pruning directs future growth thereby influencing tree shape and the type of growth produced.

(b) Regulate

Pruning regulates growth, suppressing it in unwanted areas but increasing it elsewhere, and helps regulate the number and size of fruit.

(c) Renew

Removal of spent and unproductive shoots, fruit wood and even entire branches, leaves space in the tree for new growth to take its place in a cycle of growth and cropping.

Pruning objectives

As with any activity it is important to know why you're doing it. Below are listed the principal objectives with the basic function fulfilled shown in brackets.

(a) Shape the tree to the chosen form or training system (Redirect)

Vase (see Fig 1) and central leader (see Fig 9) are common shapes, others include palmette (or 'espalier') forms (see Figs 11 and 12). Shaping involves encouraging main leading shoots in the desired direction and removing competing shoots and branches which overcrowd the tree or don't conform to the chosen shape. Manipulating the direction of growth plays a vital role in fruit development. See the next section.

(b) Limit the size i.e. height and spread of the tree (Regulate)

This helps keep fruit within reach, minimises shading of lower limbs, and restricts the tree to its allocated space in the garden. Limit tree size to a maximum of about 3 metres height and spread. Trees of this compact size are much easier to manage.

(c) Allow adequate light to penetrate through the tree (Regulate)

Removing overcrowded shoots and branches, especially near the top of the tree, results in more even growth and cropping throughout the tree.

(d) Limit fruit numbers (Regulate)

Some fruit trees if unpruned will set large numbers of fruit, many being small, misshapen and of poor colour and flavour. Overcropping often triggers a cycle of heavy and light cropping in alternate years. Heavier thinning of fruit wood in the winter preceding an expected heavy crop can help reduce this alternate cropping tendency.

(e) Remove bare and unproductive [spent] wood (Renew)

Unproductive wood with few leaf and flower buds is removed so new growth can take its place. Shoots can be shortened to a healthy leaf bud. Old and weak spur systems can be thinned out or removed completely.

(f) Renovate older and diseased trees (Renew)

To renovate older or diseased trees remove weak and diseased sections and branches. New branches when established can extend the productive life of trees.

Understanding the principles of tree growth

The growth from a particular bud depends on its position in the tree, its direction and the type and extent of any pruning, notching or bending of branches and shoots. Understand the following principles or rules and keep them in mind when pruning.

Bud position and height dominance

The strongest growth develops from buds at or near the tips, the most elevated parts of shoots and branches, and the top of the tree. A growth inhibitor produced in the leaves near the tip growth, travels down and suppresses the growth buds of lower shoots and the underside of branches. A vertical uncut shoot will grow most strongly from its tip or terminal bud. A horizontal shoot or branch will grow most strongly from buds on its upper surface, and nearer to its base (see Fig 2).

Shoot and branch angle

More upright shoots which form a narrower angle with the stem, grow more strongly, develop fewer fruit buds and are more prone to splitting at the point of attachment. Shoots growing from horizontal to 40° to 60° from the vertical are best for fruit bud formation. Growth is more uniform along the length of branches at these angles.

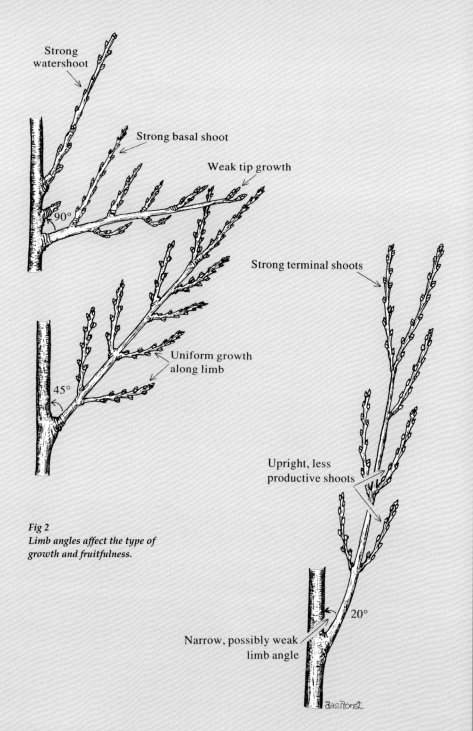

Strong
watershoot

Strong basal shoot

Weak tip growth

90°

Strong terminal shoots

Uniform growth
along limb

45°

Upright, less
productive shoots

Fig 2
Limb angles affect the type of
growth and fruitfulness.

Narrow, possibly weak
limb angle

20°

dashorst

23

The response to pruning cuts

The removal of a dominant shoot releases more vigorous growth either near or immediately below the cut. Pruning may also cause overall stunting or dwarfing. Excessive top pruning of trees results in less total growth from fewer healthy buds. Early root growth is also inhibited by removing tip buds from shoots. As a general rule, light thinning invigorates, and routine heavy shortening (heading) stunts.

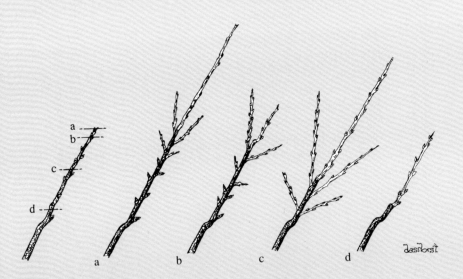

Fig 3
The result of cutting back a one year old shoot to different lengths.
(a) No cut (b) tipping (c) shortened by 1/3 to 1/2 (d) shortened to a single bud.

(a) and (b) result in moderate growth and fruit bud development; (c) and (d) result in vigorous growth and little or no fruit development that season.

Above
An example of strong spur development (pear).

Above left
Multiple bud, long lived spurs on a cherry.

Pruning guidelines – what to do and when

Deciding when to prune

Winter pruning

Routine maintenance and renewal pruning of deciduous fruit trees and vines is normally carried out during their dormant period, between the end of leaf fall (late May to early June) and bud burst (late July to September).

Trees, such as apricot and cherry, which are prone to wood diseases may be pruned during dry weather in late autumn. Never prune fruit trees during rainy weather as this is when the risk of infection by wood diseases is high.

Pruning during the growing season

Pruning during the growing season, although less widely understood and practised by home gardeners, allows added control over growth and fruiting not achieveable with winter pruning alone. Young trees can be more effectively guided and manipulated by pinching out the tips of unwanted shoots and tying down branches thereby minimising heavy winter cutting.

In cropping trees, early spring pruning allows better tree size control and light penetration with all its benefits. In vigorous trees it may be necessary to begin removing top leading shoots as early as October, to control tree height. Top pruning current seasons growth in mature trees monthly from October until the end of December is a simple way to keep trees to a manageable size of 3 metres or less without adversely affecting current or future crops.

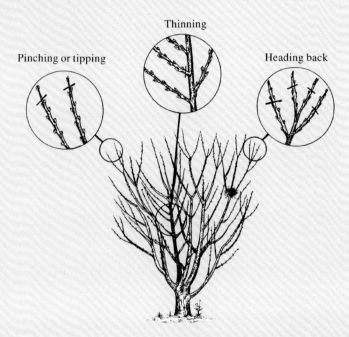

Thinning

Pinching or tipping

Heading back

Fig 4
Basic pruning cuts

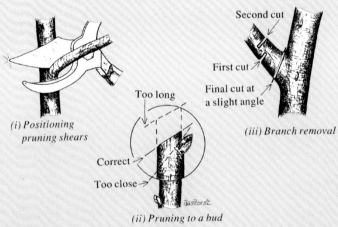

(i) Positioning pruning shears

Too long

Correct

Too close

(ii) Pruning to a bud

Second cut

First cut

Final cut at a slight angle

(iii) Branch removal

Fig 5
Making correct cuts.

Thinning involves removal of whole shoots, stems or branches to their point of origin.

Heading back is shortening of a shoot, stem or leader to a bud or side branch lower down. It is often done to stop or redirect growth.

Pinching or tipping stops growth by removing the first few buds at the end of a shoot. Very young shoots may be removed by pinching, using the forefinger and thumb.

Guidelines for most deciduous fruit trees

Shape the tree

Remove shoots or branches which do not conform to the chosen tree shape or training system. For example, in a central leader tree allow one central leading shoot only. In a vase or open centre tree remove central upright shoots.

Define the leaders

Choose a leading shoot to terminate the branch then remove all competing shoots (laterals) within 30 cm height of its tip. Remove watershoots, i.e. very vigorous upright shoots, within the tree unless one is needed to replace a main branch. Balance leader growth by shortening strong leaders and leaving moderate ones uncut.

Thin and balance lateral growth

Remove weak or spent and badly placed lateral shoots. Thin excess healthy laterals along the branches so those remaining are not less than 15 to 20 cm apart. Retain those of moderate vigour pointing outwards rather than vigorous upright shoots or those pointing to the centre of the tree.

To balance growth, vigorous well placed laterals (more than 30-40 cm long) may be shortened and weaker ones left uncut. Shorten long thin fruiting branches to an uncut lateral to stabilize them and lighten their fruit load.

Spur growth

Reduce or remove old, weak spurs in apples, pears, apricots and plums.

Dead and diseased branches

These branches may be removed at any time provided wounds are protected. The best time however is from late autumn to early spring during fine, dry weather.

Some important general points

The emphasis is on thinning

Remove some shoots and branches entirely rather than shortening many shoots. Snipping away at everything and shortening back extensively simply undermine good shoot renewal and fruit bud development. Widespread heading back is particularly detrimental in young developing trees.

Some fruits, notably grapevines and kiwifruit need heavy annual pruning to regulate growth and crop size. Others, such as figs and Japanese plums, need heavy pruning occasionally to control their excessive vigour.

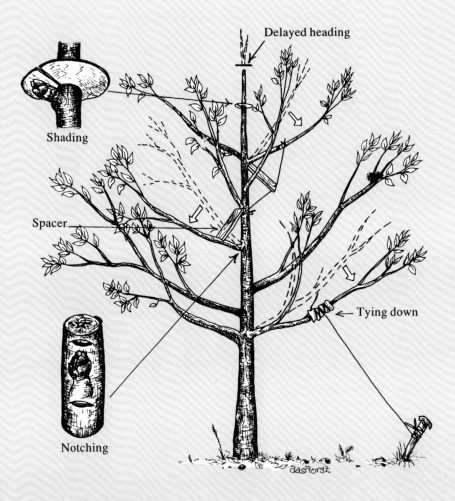

Fig 6
Some ways to direct growth.

Focus pruning at the top

and in the centre of trees to allow good light penetration to the lower parts.

Prune trees when they need it

Some, such as peach, nectarine, apricot and trellised and closely planted trees will need some regular pruning each year. Others, especially spur bearing fruits like apple, European plum and cherry, once established may need pruning only two, three, or four years out of five. In trees which tend to bear heavy and light crops in alternate years, keep pruning to a minimum following a very heavy crop.

Observation is the key

Watch your trees and take note of the way they grow and where they carry their fruit. You can learn much by doing this.

Practice, practice, practice

Don't be afraid of doing permanent damage to the tree by pruning. Remember, it's only through observation and regular practice that you will gain confidence.

To encourage growth at the desired angle

Delayed heading

Remove topmost buds or shoots in winter, or allow to grow for a few weeks in spring then remove. Subsequent growth will come at a wider angle. This technique is used in early training of young trees to induce the formation of main branches at a wider angle.

Tying down

Hold shoots or branches down with spreaders, or cords tied to a convenient anchor point.

Shading

Direct the growth of a developing bud to a lower angle by attaching a clothes peg or plastic disc on the stem just above the bud.

Notching

This involves taking out a v-shaped piece of bark. A notch above a leaf bud will allow stronger growth from the bud. A notch below the bud will result in a weaker shoot at a wider angle which may develop more fruit buds.

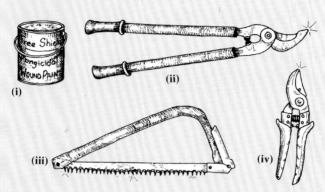

Fig 7
Basic pruning tools.
(i) Protective paint (ii) Lopping shears (iii) Bow saw (iv) Secateurs or pruning shears.

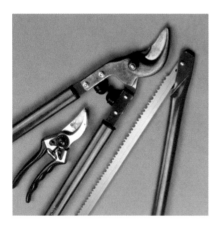

Protecting pruning cuts

All trees and woody plants have a natural ability to isolate or 'wall off' wounded tissue. This process prevents decay and disease from entering and spreading within the tree. However many fruit trees are prone to infection by some wood decay diseases entering through pruning cuts for a week or two after pruning.

Eutypa dieback or 'gummosis' *Eutypa armeniaca* attacks apricot trees and occasionally grapevines in some areas. Silverleaf *Chondrostereum purpureum*, another wood disease which can infect most deciduous fruit trees, enters through large pruning cuts.

Therefore, it is good practice to protect all pruning cuts much larger than 1 cm, especially on apricot trees. The old practice of 'sealing' cuts with

cutting green wood up to 2 cm or so in diameter (about a 5 cent coin). Lopping shears are useful for vines, heavier cuts 3-4 cm in diameter (20 cent to 50 cent coin) and cutting up prunings. A small saw is the most versatile tool for larger cuts including branches. Most pruning shears are the by-pass, scissor cut or 'parrot beak' design. An alternative is the blade-on-anvil or snap cut.

Keep your tools clean and well oiled. Never overload shears. If the branch is too thick, use a saw. Quality tools, well cared for, are an investment and should last a lifetime.

Employing others to prune your fruit trees

Your fruit trees are a valuable asset in the garden. Therefore, they need proper, or at least reasonable treatment when it comes to pruning. Should you need to employ others to prune your fruit trees or vines, gain some assurance that they will do a reasonable job and not just 'cut them back'.

Before allowing anyone to prune your fruit trees ask them for evidence of qualifications and/or experience in pruning fruit. Ask for names and telephone numbers of clients and check to find out if they are satisfied with the quality of work. If you are unsure, your fruit trees may be better left unpruned.

Should you need to employ someone who is inexperienced in pruning fruit trees and vines, gain some sound advice first (reading this book is a good start). Issue the pruner with clear instructions on what you want done, and supervise the work.

bituminous or other sealants does not necessarily prevent the entry of specific diseases. Any disease spores present in the air will settle on freshly cut surfaces immediately and most of these products do not contain a fungicide.

The recommended treatment is a liberal coating of an acrylic paint containing a freshly added fungicide to kill any fungal spores from the air which have settled on the cut and to protect the wounded area until the tree can wall it off. Use a small amount (level teaspoon) of a garden fungicide mixed into 80-100 ml of an exterior, water thinnable acrylic paint. Mix only what is needed and use it all. If you use a proprietory pruning paint, add fungicide to a small amount before use, unless the label specifically states that it contains a fungicide.

Pruning tools

It is important to have quality tools that make clean cuts and are easy to use.

Most routine pruning can be done using a pair of secateurs or pruning shears for

Training and pruning

Tree shape and training

Fruit trees can be individually trained
a number of different ways. The most
common basic shapes are central leader
and vase or open centre. A number of
variations occur between these two
basic types.

Where space is limited, other methods
can be used like multiple close planting,
palmettes and hedgerows. The method
used will depend on the tree's natural
growth habit, how well it adapts to a
system, available space, and personal
requirements and preferences.

As with any plant, early training of fruit
trees is extremely important to establish
the desired shape and to promote early
fruiting. A few minutes spent guiding
and channelling a tree's growth in the
first few years will save hours trying
to re-shape a mature tree with
heavy cutting.

Fruit trees are sold in two forms. Those
which have been headed or cut back
at 40 - 50 cm will have grown three to
five branches in the basic vase shape.
Unpruned trees will be either an
unbranched rod or branched in the
central leader form. Always purchase
trees which are in the basic desired
shape or can be adapted to suit.

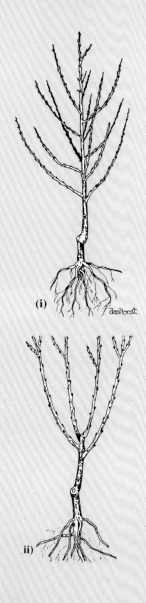

Fig 8
Two main forms of fruit tree
as purchased.
(i) Unpruned central leader tree
(ii) Vase tree headed in the nursery
to induce branching.

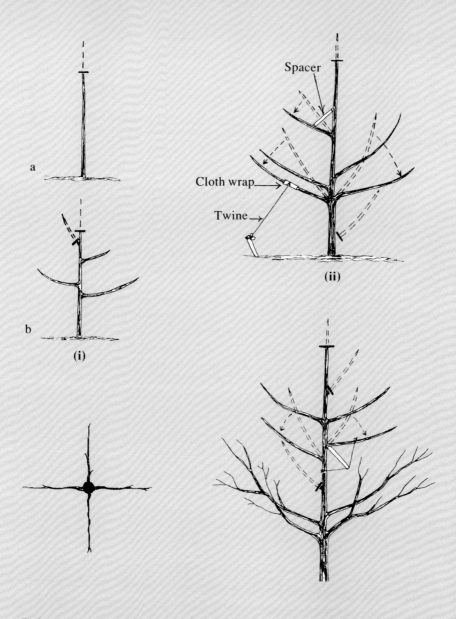

Labels on figure: Spacer, Cloth wrap, Twine

a

b

(i)

(ii)

Fig 9
Training a central leader.
(i) At planting (a) an unbranched rod
(b) branched
(ii) In winter after one year
(iii) In winter after two or more years.

Central leader

Central leader closely matches the natural growth form of many fruit trees. It is the preferred shape for most fruits except possibly apricot and some Japanese plums. The central upright stem with wide angled limbs forms a strong tree to carry heavy crops. The pyramid shape allows good light penetration to the lower limbs so trees can be planted closer, i.e. from 2.5-4 metres apart.

Central leader trees are normally established from unheaded trees either branched or unbranched. Should an unheaded tree be unavailable, select a headed tree with one strong upright branch to form the central stem.

The objectives of pruning at planting time are to define the desired tree shape and to reduce top growth to compensate for loss of roots when the tree was dug from the nursery row. If the tree has plenty of roots, top pruning is mainly for shaping. Retain the central leader uncut if possible.

Unfortunately, many nurseries overprune the roots for convenience and to save space thereby making it necessary to prune the top more heavily to compensate.

Most often the tree needs to be headed back to a length of 80-100 cm just above a healthy bud. Strong laterals positioned at 40-60 cm height may be retained to form the lower branches. If in doubt as to whether laterals are strong enough, remove all side growth to basal buds and begin with an unbranched tree.

As the tree grows, laterals will form the main branches, beginning at 40-50 cm from ground level. Branches can be arranged either in groups of 2 or 4 at intervals of 70-75 cm up the trunk, or at more or less regular intervals of 20-35 cm or so. Keep branches at an angle of at least 90 degrees to each other around the trunk to allow ladder access for pruning and harvesting. Laterals not needed for branches can be retained to carry fruit, then removed later as required.

Allow the central stem to dominate by removing any side laterals which threaten to overtake it. Keep the branches growing at a wide angle (60-75 degrees) to the stem by tying them down. Either use spacers or other methods as described on page 29 and illustrated in Fig 6. Fruit can be left on developing limbs provided its weight does not pull the branches out of shape.

Aim for a pyramid shape with the lower branches flatter and longer than the upper ones.

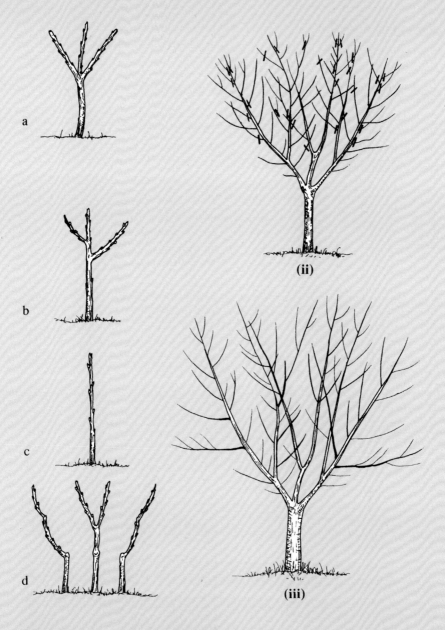

Fig 10
Training the vase or
open centre tree.

(i) Tree at planting (a) headed tree
(b) unbranched (d) multiple planting
(ii) In winter, one year after planting
showing pruning cuts
(iii) After two year's growth.

Vase or open centre

This is a common form in home gardens because it is easy to train. It is an easily trained shape for apricots and those Japanese plums which have a natural multi-leader habit. If not well managed though, it can be wasteful of space as fruit tends to be carried in its upper and outer rim due to shading of the lower parts. Trees are rather prone to branches breaking and crotches splitting under a heavy crop load and during windy conditions. In spite of these disadvantages it is still widely used.

Headed trees

At planting, select the three strongest, most evenly placed branches pointing outwards. Remove unwanted shoots. Balance growth by shortening stronger branches and leaving weaker ones either longer or uncut. Prune to outward pointing buds. About half of the top growth is removed in this process.

Unpruned trees

Select 3 to 4 strong shoots to be branches evenly spaced radially around the stem, the lowest 40 to 50 cm from the ground. Cut the stem back just above the highest branch selected at a height of about 90 to 100 cm.

Unbranched rod

If the tree is an unbranched rod or the sideshoots are few and/or weak, remove side growth and cut the rod back to 1 metre. Select suitable sideshoots for the main branches during the first growing season. Keep the chosen leaders growing at an angle of 30 to 45 degrees from the vertical by using spreaders or ties, or allow the fruit to develop and weigh the branches down. Remove or shorten shoots either close to or competing with the main leaders.

The first winter after planting remove shoots growing towards the centre of the tree, and thin laterals leaving well spaced ones about a handspan apart.

The number of branches will increase naturally from secondary leaders. If extra branching is needed shorten, the leaders by at least half in winter. The top two buds will then, typically, produce two strong shoots, doubling the number of leaders. In very vigorous growing trees, leaders can be headed back in early summer (December) to grow two extra leaders during the remainder of the season.

Multiple planting

Planting together a number of trees, usually from two to five of similar type and habit, e.g. peach and nectarine, allows several fruits to be grown in the space normally occupied by one tree. This method is easier to manage than multi-grafted trees, where one variety tends to dominate.

Trees for multiple planting can be either headed trees suitable for vase training, or unheaded with one or two strong branches on one side.

Varieties differ in their natural vigour and size. If the difference in vigor is known, plant stronger varieties to the south and weaker ones to the north to minimise shading of the weaker tree. Plant trees 30-50 cm apart. This minimises root competition in the early stages of growth and allows for trunk expansion.

Branches point outwards as with the open centre form. Leave two branches per tree if planting two trees, one or two branches with three trees, and only one branch if planting four or five trees.

Training overall is the same as for the vase or open centre form. To achieve balanced growth among the separate varieties the more vigorous trees may need tipping during the summer to prevent them from dominating.

Below
Apple trees planted in the Tatura Trellis system.

Below left
Spring blossom on pear.

Close planting in rows (hedgerow)

Small central leader trees, up to 1.5 m high, can either be planted 1.5 to 3 m apart in a row about 1 m from a boundary fence, or used as a hedge. Rows are best oriented north/south. Where row must be east/west, plant with a sunny northerly aspect, such as along a north-facing boundary. The hedgerow is limited to 3 m in height and about 1.5 m wide. Most trees suited to the central leader form can be planted this way, i.e. apple, pear, peach, nectarine and possibly some less vigorous plums.

Select either unheaded, branched or unbranched trees for planting, and position the trees so that pairs of useable strong side laterals at 40-50 cm height are directed along the row. If there is only one strong lateral remove it and start with a rod for the central leader.

As the tree grows

First season

Lateral shoots will grow on the main stem. Select the strongest of these about 60 cm apart in pairs on each side of the stem to form the main limbs, alternating 30 cm apart. Direct them along the row and keep them growing at a wide angle with the stem, i.e. about 70 to 80 degrees.

Allow the central leader to grow just ahead of the main side branches. If its growth is too vigorous and suppressing side lateral development it can be tipped to allow laterals to catch up. A top shoot can be selected later to take over as the central leader.

Retain healthy laterals not required for branches as far as possible to carry fruit. They can either be removed the following winter or treated according to the fruit type.

Second and subsequent seasons

Continue selecting laterals for main branches and maintain the central leader up to the final desired height of about 3 metres. Allow as much fruit as possible to develop on the main branches, except near the tips, to weigh them down.

The ideal final shape is a flattened pyramid. The lower limbs are longer and almost horizontal, the higher limbs are shorter with an angle of 45 to 50 degrees to the stem.

Apple trained as a Palmette on a trellis.

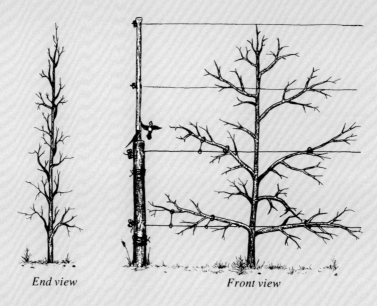

End view   *Front view*

Fig 11
*End and front view of a mature
palmette showing the trellis which
may have two, three or four wires.*

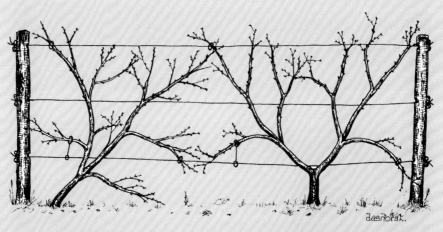

Planted at 45 degrees   *Multibranched fan*

Fig 12
*Planting trees at 45 degrees or as
a fan induces early fruiting.*

Above
*Tatura Trellis is a commercial system
where trees are planted 1 metre apart.*

Left
*Plastic tubing prevents trellis wire
damaging trunk.*

Training on a trellis

There are numerous systems or methods of growing fruit trees on trellises. Many gardeners will be familiar with espalier where branches are trained to be tied to wires in a predetermined manner. There are many possible designs, some quite elaborate.

Espalier, in its classical form, although useful for ornamentals has limited use for fruit trees. The rigid training and heavy pruning necessary results in fairly unproductive trees, and the method is generally unsuitable for stone fruits.

An alternative to espalier is the palmette system. A palmette is essentially a standard tree trained in a narrow plane with a trellis provided for support. The palmette has important advantages when compared to the classical espalier:

Light pruning results in early and consistent fruiting. Peaches and nectarines will often crop in their second year.

The informal branching structure is easy to train and manage, requiring no special skills.

In practice a palmette is very similar to closely planting trees in a hedgerow. The main difference is that branches are trained more directly along the row and on a trellis.

Training a palmette

Provide a trellis with horizontal wires spaced about 50 to 75 cm apart and plant trees 2 to 3 m apart along it. Use strong posts for the ends of the trellis and thinner wooden metal spacers or droppers between trees. Varieties with a robust branching habit, such as peach, nectarine, pear and apple, may be trained without a trellis. However the trellis is easily constructed and allows much better control in training.

Trellised trees may be either trained in a central leader form, an unheaded tree planted at 45 degrees or be a headed tree pruned to produce two to four main leaders in a fan.

Central leader

At planting, strong laterals may be retained to form the lower branches. With a weaker tree or one with small or heavily pruned roots, remove side growth and head back to a single stem at 80 to 100 cm height. As the tree grows, select laterals for branches from 50 to 70 cm apart. Laterals not required for branches can be retained to carry fruit, then removed or treated later as appropriate for the fruit type. Develop the tree to about 2.5 to 3 m in height.

Another method is to plant central leader trees at a 45° angle. Trees will develop a multileader shape. A strong vertical branch will develop from near the base. The aim is to utilize as much of the tree as possible and quickly fill the space provided.

Headed trees

Headed trees can be used to form a multileader fan. Trees such as apricots, which have a natural multileader growth habit, are better trained in this manner.

Pruning of established palmette trees follows similar guidelines to standard trees. Spring and early summer pruning is important to control vigour, and prevent shading of the lower limbs.

Stone fruits

Peach/nectarine *Prunus persica*

Originating from China (not Persia) peach, nectarine and peacharine are essentially varieties of the one species and are described here as one. Trees must have full sun and good soil drainage to thrive. All varieties are self fertile, except J H Hale (Million dollar) which needs cross pollination from another peach or nectarine.

The fungus diseases peach leaf curl and shothole are the most common problems. Use a copper based spray at leaf fall and budswell.

Training

The open centre or vase with 6 to 8 main limbs has been the main shape in the past. It is still common in domestic gardens.

The central leader, however, produces a stronger tree. Trees are also successful if multiplanted, close planted as a hedgerow or as a palmette. Closely planted trees need careful training and summer pruning to prevent shading from overcrowding.

Cropping habit

Fruit on peach is borne almost entirely on laterals, 20-40 cm long, from the previous season's growth. Fruit and leaf buds occur along the laterals individually and as triple buds, i.e. a pair of fruit buds with a single leaf bud between them.

Routine pruning

Winter Define and balance leaders and remove competition from them. Thin out weak or spent and badly placed lateral shoots.

Retain 20-40 cm long lateral shoots pointing outwards, rather than vigorous upright shoots or those pointing towards the centre of the tree. Vigorous well placed laterals over 35-40 cm in length may be shortened, especially if there are few fruit buds near the ends.

Spring/Summer Remove current season's growth to control size as desired.

Apricot *Prunus armeniaca*

Apricots like many other stone fruits originated from China. Trees grow and fruit best where summers are warm to hot and winters are cool to cold. Cropping can be less reliable where summers are cool. Blossoms come early so can be damaged by late frosts in some areas. Soils can be medium to heavy, but must be have good drainage. Plum rootstocks allow growing in heavier, wetter soils All varieties are self fertile.

Shothole disease causes holes in leaves and scabby fruit. To control, spray at leaf fall in autumn and pink-bud in spring with a copper based spray. Eutypa dieback or 'gummosis' is a serious wood disease of apricots. Refer to Protecting Pruning Cuts under Pruning Guidelines for prevention measures.

Fig 13
Dormant annual growth of peach,
apricot and almond.

(a) Lateral or longer shoot
(b) Sprig or shorter shoot
(c) Spur with flower buds
(d) Spur with leaf buds only

Peach   Apricot   Almond

Training

Apricot trees have a strong multiple branching habit. Therefore, the best way to train them is as a multiple branched vase or open centre. Multiple planting is also successful. If trellising or close planting, train as a multi-branched fan or palmette.

Apricots tend to produce long, whippy growth with narrow, weak branch attachments, and so need to be trained carefully in the first few years to establish a strong framework.

At planting, select three or four branches and cut back by at least half, or to 25 cm in length. After the first year, select the best eight evenly spaced branches in winter and cut back again by one third. The number of main leaders will then increase naturally to between 12 and 20.

Cropping habit

Fruit is borne on one year old lateral shoots, and short spurs on two to three year old wood. Apricots can set very heavy crops so it is often necessary to thin excess fruit.

Routine pruning

Once the tree shape is established, the main pruning is balancing leader growth, thinning out crowded laterals, heading back over-vigorous well placed laterals to half their length, and thinning out weak fruiting spurs. Top established trees during the spring to restrict them to no more than 3 metres.

Japanese plum *Prunus salicina*

Japanese Plums originated (despite the name) in China. Fruit is usually large, soft and juicy with red, purplish or yellow skin and yellow to deep red flesh. Trees are vigorous with rough bark and sharp-pointed leaves with smooth undersides. They thrive in hot summers and adapt to a wide range of soils when on suitable rootstocks. Most varieties require cross pollination for good crops, however some such as Santa Rosa and Satsuma are partially self fertile. Shothole can sometimes affect leaves and fruit. Spray as for apricots.

Training

Japanese plums are naturally very vigorous multi-branched trees, and are often trained as a vase with 6 to 9 main leaders. Central leader trained trees though are more compact and easy to manage. Trellising as a fan or palmette is also successful.

Some varieties like 'Santa Rosa' and 'Wickson' grow very upright, while others like 'Narrabeen' and 'Satsuma' have a more sprawling, willowy habit. Vigorous upright varieties can be opened out using spreaders and tying branches down, pruning to outward pointing wider angled laterals, and thinning out unwanted lateral growth in summer. Spreading varieties can be trained to the desired shape in their early years by pruning to more upward facing buds.

European plum

Japanese plum

Cherry

Fig 14
Dormant annual growth of European plum,
Japanese plum and cherry.

(a) Lateral or longer shoot
(b) Sprig or shorter shoot
(c) Spur with flower buds
(d) Spur with leaf buds

Cropping habit

Japanese plums flower and fruit on one year old laterals, and also on spurs which develop along the lower half of the laterals.

Routine pruning

Winter After thinning and balancing the branch leaders, head back vigorous laterals by three quarters. Spur bearing laterals of moderate vigor can be retained to crop as desired then removed, usually after they have fruited for two seasons. Thin out unproductive spurs on older wood.

Spring As trees approach the desired height, thin out unwanted shoots near the top of the tree and shorten leaders.

European plum *Prunus domestica*

The parents of modern European plums originate from Eastern Europe and Western Asia. Trees are moderate in size and prefer a cooler climate than Japanese plums but are equally adaptable to different soils. Leaves are dark green with saw-toothed edges and fine hairs underneath. Fruit is medium sized, yellow or purple skinned with firm aromatic flesh, excellent for jams and preserves and drying.

Shothole can sometimes affect leaves and fruit. Spray as for apricots.

Training

European plums with training, will form a strong framework. Young trees can be trained as a central leader, but also readily adapt to a vase or open centre form. Trellising as a palmette is also successful.

Early training mainly involves defining and balancing the primary limbs and secondary branches. Laterals greater than 40-50 cm long can be shortened by half to encourage spur formation, and to keep fruit close to the branches.

Cropping habit

Fruit is carried principally on long lived spurs which develop on two year old laterals. Fruit also develops on sprigs.

Routine pruning

Winter Retain moderately vigorous (up to 25 cm long) and less upright laterals, particularly where they occur behind, (below) spur sections. Shorten longer laterals that are over 35 to 40 cm long. Weak spurs can be thinned. Never simply shorten back all annual growth each year as this promotes vigour and delays spur formation.

Spring Thin out unwanted shoots near the top of the tree and shorten leaders to restrict tree height and width to no more than 3 metres.

Almond *Prunus dulcis*

Ancestors of the modern sweet almond grow in western Asia and Asia Minor. Normally grouped with nuts, they are botanically closely related to peaches and so culture is typical of a stone fruit. Almonds thrive in the Mediterranean type climate of southern Australia. Soils can be loam or clay-loam, even limy but drainage must be good. Cross pollination between two varieties planted close by is essential.

Shothole can affect almonds severely, causing gummy spots on fruit and shotholed leaves. Spray as for apricots.

Training

Almonds are strong trees, normally trained as an open centre with 3-4 main limbs and up to a dozen or so secondary limbs. Keep trees fairly open for good light penetration. Trees can be multiple planted for cross pollination. Trees trained as a palmette or hedge will be easier to cover with netting to protect fruit from birds.

Cropping habit

Almonds produce fruit mainly on sprigs and spurs which develop on one year old laterals and older wood. Spurs last just a few years so moderate uncut lateral growth of reasonable vigour may be retained for replacements.

Routine pruning

Once trees are established, pruning is confined mainly to thinning out weak and crowded sections during winter to encourage moderate lateral shoot growth from 15 to 25 cm long. Some thinning in the top and centre during spring & early summer will prevent overcrowding and keep the tree to a more manageable size.

Cherry *Prunus avium, P. cerasus*
(Fig 14)

Cherries come from Asia Minor in the region around the Caspian and Black Seas. For best results they need a cooler climate with a cold winter. They have a high chilling requirement and winters in many areas of southern Australia are not cold enough for long enough to produce a good crop from most cherry varieties. Trees need a good, well drained soil of reasonable depth. Cross pollination between compatible varieties is mandatory.

Cherries are most prone to Shothole, Bacterial Canker and Silverleaf. Spray thoroughly in autumn with a copper based spray and again at pink bud in early spring.

Training

Cherry trees grow naturally into large, upright trees with relatively few main limbs. To achieve a smaller easier-to-manage tree suitable for a home garden, trees are trained to an open centre vase shape with at least 8 main limbs or a central leader.

When training to a vase shape, at planting time, prune the young tree to three or four branches. To encourage wider angled shoots, prune out the top two or three shoots of the new growth in early summer. Two of the remaining shoots can then be selected for main branches.

As the tree grows, remove shoots growing towards the centre and either use spreaders or tie branches down as needed.

Cherry trees can be trained as a kind of hedge, or as either a trellised or freestanding palmette or fan.

Cropping and routine pruning

Sweet cherries

These varieties fruit almost entirely on very long lived spurs, therefore very little renewal pruning is required. Only remove overcrowded sections in winter and thin tops in spring.

Sour cherries

These fruit on short lived spurs formed on one year old wood, so moderate lateral growth is desirable. Prune after harvest, removing excess laterals and shortening those that are well placed by up to 30 cm.

Protect all pruning cuts with a fungicidal paint because cherries are very prone to both bacterial canker and silver leaf disease which enter through pruning cuts.

Blossoms are not only beautiful, they attract bees for the vital purpose of pollination. (Cherry)

Fig 15
Dormant annual growth of apple,
pear and quince.

(a) Lateral shoot
(b) Sprig or shorter shoot
(c) Flower bud or spur
(d) Leaf bud or spur

Apple   *Pear*   *Quince*

Pome fruits

Apple *Malus domestica*

Modern cultivated apples are descended from the wild crabs in the forests of Central Asia and Asia Minor. Generally, apples prefer a temperate climate, however there are numerous popular cultivars that grow and crop well in warmer areas of southern Australia. They will grow in most soils except highly alkaline and poorly drained. Numerous rootstocks are available, including dwarfing stocks. Trees need cross pollination, although single trees in a garden can produce reasonable crops given fine weather and good bee activity during flowering. Codling moth is the most important pest.

Training

Apple trees can be trained in a variety of forms or shapes. The central leader, closest to its natural shape, is easy to train, and forms a well balanced strong tree. Apples also adapt well to most other forms like palmettes and hedgerows.

Train young trees with main branches at a wide angle with the main stem as this will encourage early fruit formation which weighs branches down naturally.

Cropping habit

Apple flowers occur mainly in clusters with leaves in a compound bud. Buds develop on two year old wood and on fruit spurs, i.e. short growths carrying flowering buds on two to four year old wood. Some varieties are tip bearers, that is fruit is carried at the tips of shoots.

Routine pruning

In established fruiting trees, winter pruning involves defining the main leading branches and removing sections which have borne fruit for more than three or four years; this is to provide space for replacement growth.

In vigorous varieties, thinning out excess shoots in late spring to early summer will allow good light penetration to promote good apple skin colour, and even growth throughout the tree.

Pear *Pyrus communis*

(Fig 15)

The genus *Pyrus* ranges from Europe to China, but the ancestors of modern pears were European natives. Most of the varieties common today originate from breeding programs in France and Belgium in the period 1750-1850. Pears thrive in a temperate to Mediterranean climate and most soils (some nutrient problems can occur in very light sands) including where drainage is doubtful. Most varieties need cross pollination for best results. As with apples, codling moth is the main problem.

Training

Pears are naturally strong, vigorously growing trees. They are too large for many home gardens when allowed to grow unchecked. To allow growing in many gardens, trees must be trained and pruned to restrict size and vigour or grown on to a dwarfing quince rootstock.

Trees have a strong central leader habit and so are best trained that way.

Establish main branches up the central stem at intervals of about 30 cm and at an angle of 45 degrees or more. Allow main branches to grow uncut; fruit developing near their tips will weigh them down further.

Should the central leader grow ahead of lateral branch growth too quickly, cut it back between mid-November and mid-December. This will allow the branches to catch up and any laterals below the cut will be at a wider angle. The strongest upright shoot at the top can then be selected to continue as the central leader.

Pears, much like apples, adapt very well to trellised and freestanding forms. Easiest to manage for home garden fruit growing is the palmette with either oblique or horizontal arms. Freestanding trees can be trained in this way but a trellis allows better control. Keep pairs of branches spaced at 70 to 75 cm apart up the main stem.

Cropping habit

Pears produce clusters of flowers with leaves from mixed buds in a similar manner to apples. On young trees some flowering buds will form near the tips of one year old laterals, and spurs will develop on older wood. On older trees flowering buds develop at the base of one or two year old shoots. Extensive spur systems can develop on older wood that is not too shaded.

Routine pruning of established trees

Define the main leaders, then thin out unwanted shoots near the top of the tree. Thin out shoots along the branches spacing them not less than 20 cm apart.

Pears can crop very heavily on spurs on older wood. Thin out excessive spurs to reduce fruit numbers and increase quality if desired. Top pruning during spring and early summer will be necessary to control tree height.

Nashi or Asian Pear *Pyrus pyrifolia*

The sand pear, nashi or Asian pear comes from central China and Japan. The often apple shaped fruit has a crisp texture, much like an apple and is more an alternative to apples than the soft, melting flesh of European pears. Trees are very similar in shape and habit to European pears and require similar care. Cross pollination is with European and other nashi varieties. Fruit should be allowed to ripen fully on the tree.

Training and Pruning

Nashi trees are vigorous central leader trees much like European pear; they are trained and pruned in a similar manner. Trees may be trained as a central leader or as a palmette. Flowers and fruit are carried mainly on two to three year old wood, and at the tips of one year old laterals.

Routine pruning is much like that for European pear. Define main leading branches in winter. During spring and early summer, thin out excess shoots particularly near the top of the tree to control tree size.

Quince *Cydonia oblonga*

(Fig 15)

The common quince has been cultivated for thousands of years from it's origins in northern Persia and Armenia. They grow readily in a range of climates and soils. They can bear heavily so some fruit thinning may be desirable. Quinces are self pollinating.

Quince trained as a classical espalier.

Training

Quinces grow naturally into dense bushy trees with multiple branching. Trees can be trained as a vase, central leader, hedge or trellised as a palmette. A simple method for a free standing tree is a central leader with radiating main branches.

Early training involves defining the main limbs and, in winter, thinning out excess shoots which sometimes develop on the ends of branches. Quinces sucker freely so these should be removed as they appear.

Cropping habit

Fruit is borne from large single white or pink flowers which emerge from the tips of short shoots produced during spring. Trees tend to overcrop and break branches, so remove excess fruit if desired.

Routine pruning

Prune to keep the tree open to control sucker and watershoot growth. In winter, thin out overcrowded, spindly shoots and whippy shoots which develop on the ends of branches. In spring and early summer, thin tops to control height and remove excess tip shoots.

Vines

Grapevines *Vitis vinifera*

(Figs 16, 17 and 18)

The grape is one of the most ancient and widely cultivated of fruits. Originating in the area between the Black and Caspian seas, the fruit is used for eating, drying and of course wine.

Grapevines are extremely tough and will adapt to a range of climates, but those with warm, dry summers are preferred. Vines have a deep root system and will grow in most soils. Inflorescences are fully self fertile. The main disease problems encountered by gardeners are powdery mildew which only requires humidity and overcast conditions, and downy mildew which needs periods of steady rain on young growth.

Grapevines can be trained in a variety of ways. The main requirements are that the annual growth receives full sun and the wood from which it comes occurs roughly at one level. In the home garden, grapevines are normally trained as a two arm espalier to a single wire at a height of 1.2 - 1.4 metres. A second wire 40 - 60 cm above the first is an option to support the annual growth. Space young vines 1.5 to 3 m apart according to the vigour of the variety, micro climate and soil.

Training the young vine

When planting rooted cuttings or grafted vines, retain the strongest shoot only and cut it back to two or three buds in length. A string from the main support to the young plant will provide purchase and support for the young shoot.

Forming the trunk

During the first growing season, as the young vine grows, select the strongest main leading shoot (often from the topmost bud) and train it vertically towards the wire or top of the structure to which it is to be trained. Tip prune other shoots periodically to keep them short. If the shoot reaches 10 to 15 cm above the wire or trellis by January, pinch out the tip to force out lateral growth. If not, allow to grow uncut.

The first winter

Shorten the main leading shoot back to where it has achieved 8 - 10 mm thickness. This may be to the wire on a 1 m high trellis or half way up a pergola post with a vigorous plant. If growth has been weak the first year, cut right back to a three bud spur near ground level. There is nothing to be gained by retaining weak wood. Remove completely all growth not required for training, particularly from the main stem.

The second growing season

Forming the main arms

When the main leading shoot reaches trellis height, take out the tip to stimulate lateral growth. This is then trained along the trellis as desired to form the main arms of the vine. Train shoots directly along the trellis. Never wrap or wind shoots around posts or wires as they will become constricted as they expand with age.

Establishing spurs

Spurs are established on the main arms, usually the winter following their second season. At winter pruning, select

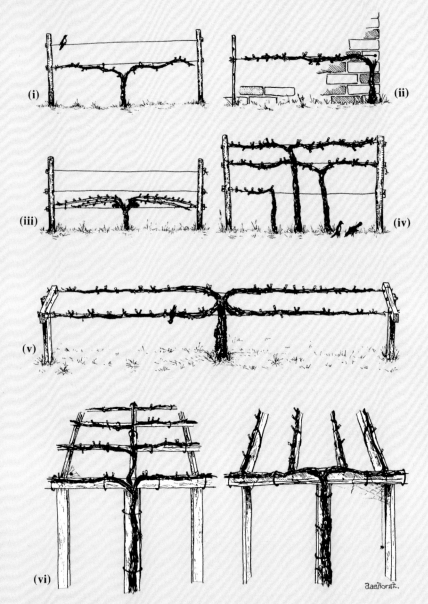

Fig 16
Some ways to train grapevines.

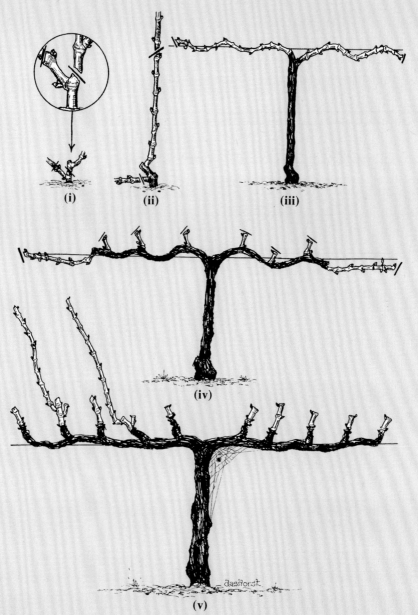

Fig 17
Training a grapevine.   *Shown in winter after pruning: (i) at planting*
(ii) when main shoot reaches wire
(iii) arms formed
(iv) spurs defined
(v) mature vine: LHS-rods and spurs; RHS-spurs only.

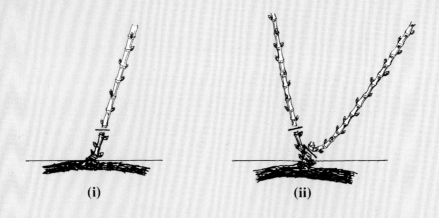

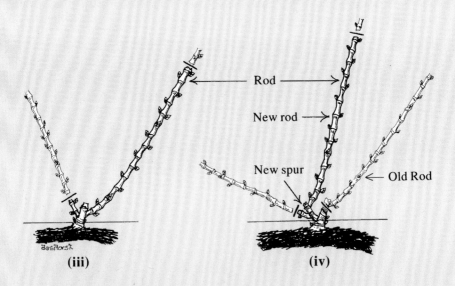

Rod

New rod

New spur

Old Rod

Fig 18
Pruning grapevines in winter
[no incidental growth shown].

(i) Establishing spur on a main arm
(ii) Pruned back to a single spur after one season
(iii) pruned to rod and spur
(iv) routine winter pruning of rod and spur

canes 25-40 cm apart growing upright from the main arms and shorten them back to two buds, counting from the base of the cane. Ignore any basal buds.

Spurs are the starting point for all fruiting wood and are renewed each year. Weak spurs can be cut out at any time and a strong nearby cane selected and cut to two buds to replace it.

The vine can be extended or reduced at any time to achieve the desired dimensions. Unwanted or encroaching shoots can be tipped or headed back anytime and removed the following winter.

Pruning established grapevines

Grapevines flower and fruit on the current season's growth from buds on last season's canes. Shoots growing directly from older wood such as the trunk and main arms produce few flowers and fruit.

The aim in grapevine pruning is to allow for enough fruitful shoots to develop each year for a good crop and to keep vegetative growth to an acceptable level. Grapevines are pruned very hard compared to fruit trees. Up to 90% or more of the last season's growth is removed at pruning. Unpruned vines will eventually become a tangle of fruitless growth.

Many grapevines fruit well on shoots from buds near the base of last season's canes and are pruned to spurs 2 or 3 buds in length. In some varieties, the lower buds do not produce fruitful shoots. In these varieties longer canes or rods are left to bear fruit while spurs provide for replacement wood. Table

grape varieties requiring cane or rod and spur pruning include 'Sultana', (also called 'Thompson Seedless'), 'Calmeria', 'Ohanez', 'Crimson Seedless', Fantasy Seedless', 'Red Globe', 'Ruby Seedless' and others. 'Purple Cornichon' and 'Muscatel' can be spur pruned, but often yield more fruit when some 6-8 node rods are left. 'Emperor' can be pruned to 6-8 rods of 10 nodes or all 4 bud spurs.

(a) Spur pruning

To establish spurs in winter, select upright canes about 25 to 30 cm apart on the main arms and shorten them back to 2 or 3 buds.

Remove all other canes and growth entirely, including watershoots and suckers from the trunk. The next season each bud on the spur produces a long shoot (cane) on which the bunches of grapes are carried.

The following winter, the old spur is cut back leaving only the cane from the lowest bud which is then pruned back to 2 buds to form the new spur.

(b) Cane or rod and spur pruning

Training

Cane or rod pruned vines can be trained as either an espalier or over a pergola as with spur pruning. In addition to spurs, a number of rods are left to carry fruit.

Where the vines are to be closely planted, principally for fruit, or where vine vigour is low, such as in cool climates, the 'Systéme Guyot' can be used. The permanent arms are kept very short, 30 cm or less. Two to four rods from 9 to 12 buds long, as well as spurs, are established on each arm.

Pruning

In rod and spur pruning, establish two bud spurs as in spur pruning. These will produce a long cane from each bud. In winter, shorten the cane from the upper bud to 7-12 buds long (depending on the variety) to form the rod, then shorten the cane from the lower bud to 2 buds to form a spur. During the following growing season the rod carries fruit and the spur produces two vigorous canes. The following winter the old rod is cut out, and the canes on the spur are pruned to form the new rod and spur as described above.

Mature vines, depending on age, size and vigour can carry from 4 to 10 rods and spurs, plus as many additional single spurs as required.

Kiwifruit vines growing on T-trellises.

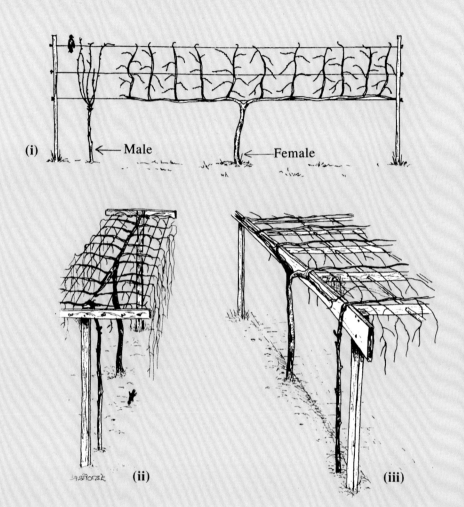

(i) ← Male   ← Female

(ii)   **(iii)**

Fig 19
Ways to train kiwifruit vines.
(i) Fence (ii) T-trellis (iii) Pergola.

Kiwifrut (Chinese Gooseberry)
Actinidia deliciosa

(Figs 19 and 20)

Kiwifruit is the name coined in New Zealand for the brown, egg-shaped fruit of the vine native to the Yang-tse valley in southern China. Vines grow well in milder parts of southern Australia. Ideal soil is a neutral to slightly acidic sandy loam and good drainage but medium loams with slightly alkaline to neutral pH are acceptable.

Kiwifruit grow into vigorous long lived vines which need a strong trellis, and regular pruning to control their rampant growth and to achieve a balance with fruit production. Kiwifruit vines are dioecious, that is some plants produce only male flowers, and others only female flowers. In cultivation, one male can provide pollen for up to 8 females.

Male plants are required only to provide pollen for female plants. Train the vine on a single stem to trellis height, then maintain the plant as a single head without arms. Each year in spring, after flowering has finished, prune back hard to short spurs.

Female vines are planted 5-7 metres apart and can be trained in a similar manner to grapevines as follows:

(a) A two or three wire fence 1.8 m high with wires at 1, 1.4 and 1.8 m height. The main arms are trained along the bottom wire, and the fruiting arms and annual growth respectively across the second and third wires.

(b) A T-trellis with posts 1.8 m high and crosspieces 1.2 m long. The main arms are trained along the central wire and the fruiting arms across wires between the ends of the crosspieces.

(c) A pergola with horizontal wires 60 cm apart across the rafters. The main arms are trained along the main beam of the pergola, and the fruiting arms and foliage across the wires.

The T-trellis and pergola are preferred where space permits. The 2 or 3 wire fence needs regular attention to keep it under control and can be a challenge to maintain.

Training

Plant young vines directly below the main support wire or at the base of the pergola post. Train the strongest shoot up to the wire or main beam of the pergola. Nip the tip of the main shoot, then select the top two shoots and train along the trellis to form the two main arms. Tie the arms down flat. Kiwifruit vines have a twining habit and tend to constrict when wrapped around posts or wires.

The fruiting arms are branched sideshoots spaced 30 to 40 cm apart along the main arms.

Cropping habit

Kiwifruit are borne on the first three to six buds of the current season's growth arising from one year old wood. Shoots arising from the one year old main arms on a new vine will fruit the first year. Shoots arising from older main arms or the trunk will not fruit but produce fruiting laterals the following year.

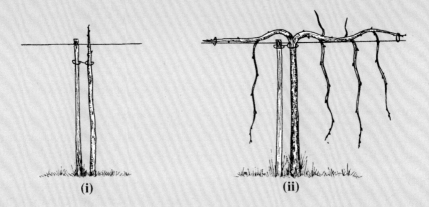

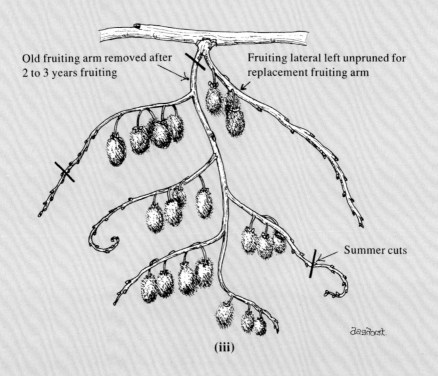

Old fruiting arm removed after 2 to 3 years fruiting

Fruiting lateral left unpruned for replacement fruiting arm

Summer cuts

dashorst

(iii)

Fig 20
Pruning and training kiwifruit.

(i) A single shoot trained to the support wire or pergola
(ii) The next season permanent main arms grow:
select laterals for fruiting arms
(ii) Detail of fruit arm showing pruning cuts

To keep the vines open and yielding good sized fruit, regular pruning is necessary. The following pruning instructions refer to female plants.

Winter pruning (June - July)

Cut out completely fruiting arms which have carried fruit for two or more seasons. Leave a replacement shoot at or near the base. Remove all unwanted canes from the main arms and watershoots from the trunk.

Summer pruning

Summer pruning is carried out every six or eight weeks to curb excessive shoot growth, and to allow good light penetration so energy goes to fruit development.

Shorten fruit bearing laterals to two or three buds past the last fruit, and cut back the vigorous shoots from the main arms to one or two buds in length. New shoots from these will be less vigorous and more suitable as replacement fruiting laterals.

Passionfruit *Passiflora edulis*

The black or purple passionfruit is a subtropical evergreen climbing vine from Brazil.

It needs a warm, sheltered, sunny site facing north or east and will tolerate only very mild frost. Seedlings must have well drained soil. Grafted varieties have greater tolerance of soil conditions. Plant in spring. Vines produce their best crops when well fertilised and watered. Passionfruit vines have a limited productive life due to the constant threat from woodiness virus for which there is no remedy. Infected vines are simply removed and replaced.

Flowering and fruiting

Flowers and fruits are born on current season's growth. Flowers are self pollinating, but are receptive to pollen for a short period only. They require mild, fine morning weather and bees for a good fruit set. Hand pollination helps fruit set in cooler weather and climates. Fruit matures in about three months.

Training

As with all vines, passionfruit needs trellis support. It can be up to 2 metres high and at least 3 metres long It can be mesh or single, horizontal wires.

Train a single leading shoot up a thin stake or suspended string to the bottom trellis wire. Then pinch the shoot tip to encourage side shoots along the wire. Train the leading shoot up and lay down side shoots at 30-50 cm intervals up the trellis.

Pruning

Regular pruning is important to keep vines compact and productive. Unpruned vines quickly become an unproductive, tangled mass of old and new growth. Prune established vines in late winter or early spring. Shorten all lateral shoots to 20-30 cm length. Any existing shoots and flowers removed at pruning will be quickly replaced. During the season, tie back fruiting shoots and remove unwanted excess growth. Older and overgrown vines can be cut back with hedging shears, then trimmed to side shoots. Older main stems can be removed periodically and replaced with new shoots. The broad aim is to maintain new growth and fruiting close to the framework of the vine.

Evergreens

Citrus *Citrus spp.*

The citrus we know and love originated in south and south-east Asia. Most need a warm, frost free climate and sandy to loamy soils with excellent drainage. They are mostly self pollinating.

Trees grow naturally into bushy trees with little formal training and will initially crop well. However, eventually trees will become overgrown with dense, unproductive and spent wood. When trained, shaped and pruned, trees will be healthier, easier to manage and produce more reliable and consistent crops of good sized and well coloured fruit throughout their productive life.

Some facts

Citrus trees have a productive life of 20-30 years. After this, vigour often declines, fruit becomes smaller and nutritional problems, pests and diseases make trees difficult to manage.

The most productive growth and fruiting occurs in the outer 90 cm of the tree canopy, so optimum canopy size need be no more than 2-3 metres. A large sprawling canopy takes up a lot of space and produces no more fruit than a compact well managed one.

The number of terminal (tip end) shoots determines fruit numbers. More shoot tips result in more fruit, directing tree vigour into producing fruit rather than excess growth. Regulating the number of shoot terminals is the best way to achieve a balance between growth and fruit numbers.

Young trees and shaping

Retain three to four main branches 50-70 cm above ground level at time of planting. As the young tree grows, tip prune young shoots to keep the tree compact. The ideal shape is a flat topped pyramid. Maintain roughly this shape by tipping shoots and shortening back over-vigorous watershoots in late winter. This early and continuous shaping minimises heavy cutting later on.

Maintaining healthy mature trees

Mature trees should be little more than 3 metres high and the base of the leaf canopy 2-2.5 metres across and 75-100 cm above ground level (see illustration opposite). This shaping will maximise light penetration through the tree and multiple shoot terminals to bear fruit.

Such trees remain healthier and more productive with less dead wood, fewer disease and pest problems, are less prone to wind damage and are more compact and accessible for harvesting, pruning, spraying, watering, weeding and mulching.

Citrus trees respond well to shaping. Trim untidy growth to produce the desired shape. The best time is after harvest in spring. Early pruning will promote early summer growth that will be mature before the summer heat and the arrival of pests such as citrus leaf miner.

Fruiting citrus trees carry their flowers mainly on the new spring growth flush, except for lemons which also flower on their late summer to autumn growth. Consequently as the tree grows, much of the fruit is carried towards its outer parts. As trees mature they may become dense and twiggy with spent fruiting shoots. To avoid this, when harvesting the fruit pick it with a long stem up to 10 cm or so long and back to a healthy side shoot. Then snip off the stem at the fruit button. This way, spent fruiting shoots do not accumulate in the tree (see Fig 21).

Overgrown trees

There are many established trees in gardens which although sound, are overgrown with much dead and leafless wood inside the canopy. These can be reconstructed after harvest or in late winter. Initially cut out all dead and leafless wood, then work towards the recommended shape using secateurs, hedge clippers or a saw as needed.

Very old (over 25-30 years) weak and disease and pest affected trees may be induced to crop for a few more years by skeletonizing back to branchlets about thumb thickness. Old trees like this however are at the end of their productive life and often are better removed and /or replaced.

The branches of hedged and skeletonized trees are prone to sunburn. To prevent this, before summer, paint the trunk and main branches with a cheap, water-based white house paint, or if desired, a whitewash available from commercial horticultural suppliers.

Loquat *Eriobotrya japonica*

Loquats are subtropical evergreen trees from the Himalayas, eastern Asia to eastern Malesia. Trees can grow over

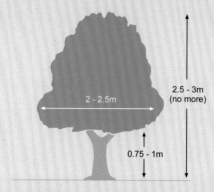

Healthy mature citrus tree shape

2.5 - 3m
(no more)

2 - 2.5m

0.75 - 1m

Fig   Persimmon   Citrus

Fig 21
Growth of fig, persimmon and citrus.   *(a) Immature fruit which will mature*
early the following summer.
Persimmon: (b) fruit buds (c) leaf buds.
Citrus: when harvesting cut stem at
(d) then at (e), discard stem piece.

6 metres tall, but much smaller when grown on quince rootstock. They have attractive, large, dark green leaves with downy undersides and yellow, sweet fruit with three or four large seeds. Trees prefer a warm climate, but once established can tolerate moderate frosts. The preferred soil is neutral to acid loam to clay-loam. Although tolerant of dry conditions trees need adequate water to achieve good fruit size.

Flowering and Fruiting

Unlike most other fruits, loquats flower from late autumn and into winter in clusters of 50 or more creamy, slightly scented flowers at the end of the current season's growth. Flowers are self-fertile. Trees tend to overcrop with small fruit leading to cropping only every second year. To avoid this, thin flower clusters, leaving no more than 3 to 5 flowers per cluster. Fruit ripens in spring.

Training

Trees grow naturally with a short trunk and multiple branches. Train young trees with three to five main branches spaced at between 50-100 cm height. Then leave trees until they commence fruiting at four or five years.

Pruning

Prune after harvest (late spring or early summer) once the tree is fruiting and approaches 2 metres or so in height and spread. Thin out excess terminal (tip) shoots to allow good light penetration and regulate fruit numbers. For ease of management, keep the tree to no more than 3 metres or so high.

Other deciduous fruits

Fig *Ficus carica*

The fig is another ancient fruit from western Asia and Asia minor. Very adaptable, trees will grow and fruit from subtropical to temperate climates and most soil conditions. As with most fruit trees, regular watering and some fertiliser is desirable. Varieties commonly available are self fertile.

Figs trees are usually trained to a multibranched vase. A newly planted tree may be headed from 60 to 75 cm height and about three lateral shoots retained to form main branches. Trees may also be trained as a hedge or trellised as a multibranched fan.

Cropping habit

Varieties of the common or Adriatic fig may produce two crops of fruit per year. The first crop in spring and early summer, forms nearer the tips of previous season's growth and ripens in early summer. The second and main crop forms towards the base of current season's growth and ripens in autumn.

Pruning

If your tree regularly produces a good quality first crop, retain mature fig bearing shoots in winter to mature the following early summer. To increase the quality of the first crop, pinch out the new shoot tips at the end of these branches to divert nutrients to the developing crop.

To stimulate strong new growth and a good main crop, shorten the most recent shoots by half to two thirds in winter, thereby removing the first crop. Thin out long, spindly and overcrowded shoots but always cut back to a joint or side shoot as headed shoots often die back.

Heading vigorous fruit bearing shoots in summer may encourage the crop to mature earlier.

Older overgrown trees that make little shoot length may be heavily thinned and headed back in winter to stimulate vigorous new growth and fruit the following season.

Mulberry *Morus nigra M. alba, M. rubra*

Mulberry trees, like figs are deciduous, naturally hardy, adaptable, drought tolerant trees, but need some care for best results. Three varieties available are Black English, Hicks Fancy and Downings Everbearing.

Mulberries are monoecious, they produce separate male and female flowers on the same tree. Male flowers occur in long pendulous catkins on new spring growth. The fruit forms from the swollen female inflorescences near the base of the male catkins.

Mulberry trees may be trained as a central leader, modified central leader or vase. Hedge or palmette is also successful. Once the basic tree shape is established the main routine pruning is to regulate tree size. This can be carried out after fruiting or during the winter dormant season.

Japanese Persimmon *Diospyros kaki*

The persimmon is a deciduous subtropical tree native to China and introduced into Japan in the 8th Century. Trees grow and crop well in southern Australia. They have a strong taproot which must not be damaged at planting.

The tree has a rounded multi-branching habit and can be trained initially as a central leader with several evenly spaced branches. Shorten the central leader by 1/3 each winter to encourage adequate side branches to form. The centre will open out naturally as the tree grows. Persimmons also adapt well to training on a trellis as a palmette.

Cropping habit

In the persimmon, only the top two or three buds from last season's growth will produce flowering shoots (see Fig 21). Flowers and fruit develop near the base of the current season's growth. When the new growth has matured in late spring, flowers emerge on short stalks in the leaf axils, i.e. where the leaf joins the shoot.

Routine pruning

The bearing position on established persimmon trees gradually extends further from the centre of the tree leading to long thin unproductive shoots which fruit only at the tips. These bend and droop under the weight of foliage and fruit, and are prone to wind damage.

To overcome or avoid this, leave unpruned many shoots carrying vigorous well formed buds to grow next season's fruiting shoots. Then cut back some less vigorous shoots to two or three buds in length. From these buds vigorous shoots will develop the following spring, which in turn will carry fruiting shoots the following season.

Further reading

Books (some of these are out of print, but still relevant)

Anthony Allen, *Growing Nuts in Australia*. Night Owl Publishers 1987.

Paul Baxter, *Growing Fruit in Australia*. Nelson 1981, 1987; Pan Macmillan 1990, 1998.

Louis Glowinski, *The Complete Book of Fruit Growing in Australia*. Lothian 1991, 1997.

Kevin Handreck, *Gardening Down-under*. CSIRO 1993, 2001.

Susanna Lyle, *Discovering Fruit and Nuts*. Landlinks Press 2006.

Clive Stone, *The Australian Berry Book*. Pioneer Design Studio 1978, 1981, 1992.

Internet

The following is just a sample of the vast information resources available from the internet.

Australian Citrus Growers Inc.
http://www.austcitrus.org.au/

Home Citrus Growers
http://www.homecitrusgrowers.co.uk/

Rare Fruit Society of South Australia
http://www.rarefruit-sa.org.au/

Flemings Nurseries
http://www.flemings.com.au/

SA Research & Development Institute
http://www.sardi.sa.gov.au/

Victorian DPI Notes Information Series
http://www.dpi.vic.gov.au/

WA Department of Agriculture & Food
http://www.agric.wa.gov.au/

Queensland DPI
http://www.dpi.qld.gov.au/